The Prestige Ser

Sheffield United Tours

A Brief History

Trevor Weckert

© 2007 Venture Publications Ltd

ISBN-10 1 905304 14 5
ISBN-13 978 1 905304 14 1

Cover: At Davenport Rugby League ground in Stockport is No. **337** (**337 EWJ**), the first of nine 2U3RA Reliances. This rather imposing view shows the 44-seat version.

Rear Cover: A Windover Kingsway AEC Regal IV featured on the cover of the 1953 brochure with the backdrop of 'The Gay Coachman' Inn.

Inside front cover: This picture seems to sum up SUT. No. **226** (**PWB 226**), 'Gay Elizabethan', an immaculate Regal IV pre-selector with Windover Kingsway coachwork, featuring 30 reclining seats and toilet in its rear entrance body. New in 1953, it is seen parked on the road just outside the garage prior to naming. (*Tom Robinson)* De-licensed for the winter in the garage yard is No. **369** (**KWE 369D**). The grill/headlight panels were repainted red after first repaint. However, I personally thought they looked better in original grey. (*Paul Beardsley*)

Inside rear cover: Various coaches over the years were painted in a blue and grey livery, some for use on SWFC football contract, but this was not always the case. Here No. **350** (**AWA 350B**) is seen displaying such colours and carrying a modified, shallower side trim. (*Paul Beardsley*)

The last vehicles in the fleet to carry the familiar red and grey livery were 417-24 (NWB 417-24K) new in 1972. These signalled the end of a long tradition of Plaxton products for the company. No. **419** is seen prepared in Charlotte Road for use as a mobile advertisement for SUT. Five of this batch were later leased to London Country in 1980. (*B Ridge*)

Title page: Despite the fact that SUT coaches could be found on tour all over Europe, Blackpool was perhaps the destination chosen by the majority of the company's customers over the years. An AEC Reliance with distinctive Burlingham Seagull bodywork is seen at the Coliseum Coach Station.

Below: Most of the early Kitson fleet is seen here parked on Herries Road in Sheffield with the famous 'Five Arches' in the background. Among the line up are: **WE 2282** - Leyland Lion PLSC3, **NU 9321** - Lancia, **CC 3010** - Leyland 'G', **WA 4892** - Leyland S5, **DB 2102** - Leyland, **CC 3011** - Leyland 'G', **FR 7262** - Lancia and **WE 1709** - Leyland PLSC3. As can be seen, varying adaptations of Kitson's blue and white livery are in evidence.

WINDOVERS LIMITED

BY APPOINTMENT TO HIS MAJESTY THE KING. COACHBUILDERS

COACHWORK SPECIALISTS

SINCE 1796

The "Huntingdon"

The Windover Body, supplied to the order of Sheffield United Tours, on A.E.C. Chassis
which was awarded first prize in the International Coach Rally at Montreux in June.

THE HYDE, HENDON, LONDON, N.W.9

TELEPHONE COLINDALE 4031-2-3-4

Windovers Limited of Hendon was rightly proud of its association with SUT and used the success of the
company prominently in this advertisement from the April 1950 issue of *Bus & Coach*. Similar bodies
were supplied to many large fleets but the unseasoned timber from which the frame was constructed (all
that was available at the time) meant that many had fairly short lives. (*STA*)

THE SUT STORY

Sheffield United Tours Limited (SUT) was one of the most prestigious coach companies within the British Electric Traction Group (BET). Indeed, it was one of Britain's most respected coach tour operators. Employees would say it was like working for a family business and they felt part of the team. For the 40 years of its existence, customers would return each year to travel on the familiar red and grey coaches. Often people would book a tour based on the courier allocation rather than any particular location, such was the relationship between client and staff. The origins of the company go back to when Arthur Kitson, coach proprietor of Westmoreland Street, Sheffield, decided to sell off his coaching interests to the BET. Kitson had previously operated bus services within the city in addition to his excursion activities. He had commenced trading following the end of World War 1, a limited company being formed on 31st December 1926. On the 18th December 1934, the entire shareholding was acquired by the Yorkshire Traction Co Ltd, who in turn resold half their share to East Midland Motor Services. The new limited company came into effect on 1st January 1935. Other local coach operators were purchased shortly afterwards,

including some who had pooled their operations under the 'United Motor Services' title. John Grocock, of Ellesmere Road, who also ran a removal business, haulage company and fruit and vegetable shops, in addition to his coaching interests, had the latter acquired and was integrated into the new fleet during January 1935. At the same time, Ernest Warriner of Rock Street and Harvest Lane, George Thomas Nicholson of Burns Road and Hancock's Motor Tours of Bamford in Derbyshire were all engulfed into this rapidly expanding fleet. One month later, the enterprise of Jack & Wilfred Kavanagh of Blonk Street succumbed. Alone of these proprietors, AF Hancock was to become a director of SUT.

The title of 'Sheffield United Tours' was adopted to reflect the encompassing of the various fleets and came into effect on 1st March 1935. Previously, the name adopted was that of Arthur Kitson Ltd. During May of that year, the coaching interest of W Caudle of Queens Road, Sheffield was purchased. Shortly after these takeovers, the North Western Road Car Co challenged East Midland Motor Services and Yorkshire Traction on the grounds that neither company was Sheffield based, merely running services into the city. Since North Western was in a similar position, it argued that it was entitled to an equal share, and so

Driver Harold Pearson stands proudly in front of **RA 8675**, an Albion PNC26 of Hancock's fleet. This 25-seater never entered service with SUT. It was new in 1929.

eventually it was agreed to divide the shareholding equally between the three companies. The combined SUT fleet at this time totalled 71 coaches and had cost £101,000. During April of 1936, a Rotherham-based company, Harold Barker of Doncaster Gate, was taken over. In March of the following year, 1937, A & L Bailey of Earsham Street, Sheffield was taken over. At the same time, a new purpose-built garage was opened at Charlotte Road to accommodate this enlarged fleet. Prior to this, vehicles had been garaged at various depots within the city which had been acquired along with the businesses, including the Pond Hill depot of Kitson and the Sheffield bases of Hancock's which were at Church Lane and Old Hall Road. Despite the outbreak of war in September 1939, the tours and excursions continued to operate almost as normal, right through the 1940 season. Severe air raids the following year brought the programme to a halt, many coaches being requisitioned by the military. Eight coaches were loaned to Crosville Motor Services, while some of those that remained were used on workmen's services. Some never returned to their home city whilst others were repurchased later, most of which were in a very sorry state, but supplies of new coaches were not readily available so a hasty patching up job was needed.

After the hostilities, an attempt was made to return the fleet to the carriage of pleasure traffic but inevitably this took some time. Although SUT had been registered during 1935, it was initially decided to operate all tours under the 'Hancock's Motor Tours' title whilst express and excursions were marketed under the 'United Motor Services' banner. It was not until after the war that all operations came under the 'Sheffield United Tours' heading and the pre-war titles were eventually abandoned. Express service got off to a relatively humble start after the war, operating to Blackpool, Cleethorpes, Morecambe, Scarborough, Skegness and Southport. This was developed to feature more and more destinations as the years progressed. SUT's holiday tours programme was extensive, comprising both British and Continental tours and although the latter had been offered before the war under the Hancock's Motor Tours banner, it was not until 1949 that such tours really took off. In that year, three Continental holidays were offered. By the following year, five Continental, together with 17 British tours were advertised in the brochure. An opportunity had been taken in 1951 to operate a tour to the Festival of Britain which was located on the south bank of the River Thames in London. Passengers travelled there in one of the Windover Kingsway 'Gay' class

Built in 1926 for AF Hancock in whose fleet we see **NU 9428**, an Albion PFA26 with Buckingham 20-seat body.

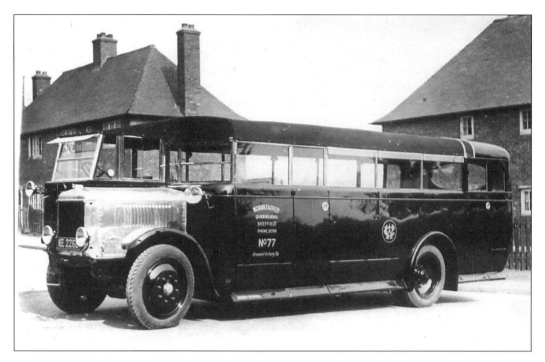

Above: One of the constituent companies which is still extant today, albeit as a removals business, is that of W Caudle Limited. Pictured here, by its coachbuilder when new in 1928, with its red paintwork gleaming, **WE 2268** is a Karrier with bodywork by Reeve & Kenning. It was taken into SUT stock but not operated.

Below: George Nicholson was one of the original consortium being taken over in January 1935. Leyland Cub KP3 was painted in deep red and registered **WJ 4039**. The coach was new in May 1932 and when sold in March 1938 it went to OR Williams (Whiteways) of Waenfawr.

Wearing the smart chocolate/maroon livery is John Grocock's **WJ 6502**, a Leyland TS4 with locally built Cravens coachwork pictured on Richmond Road. The 'Ellesmere Tours' title was Grocock's trading name. (*Cravens*)

coaches. Once there, you could view, along with every other visitor, another of SUT's 'Gay' clan in the shape of NWB 199 which was an exhibit in the transport section of the Exhibition. The same year saw the introduction of 'Stay at Home Tours'. For five consecutive days (Monday to Friday) you travelled on a different tour each day, returning home each evening. Destinations featured not too distant locations such as York, Whitby, Scarborough, Southport and Hathersage, all for the grand total of 5 guineas (1 guinea equalled £1 1s pre-decimalisation; £1.05 today).

The company had set its sights on further takeovers but this was not to occur until the early 'fifties. An operator who had been good competition for SUT in the pre-war years was Abbey Lane Motor Services trading as 'Beauchief Coaches'. This company had been founded in December 1930 and expanded quickly by acquiring Brooks & Senior of Abbeydale Road in May 1933. Further expansion of this company took place in May 1936 when Samuel Bernard Hogg of Pitsmoor Road was purchased. Through these acquisitions, Beauchief Coaches had acquired very lucrative services to Llandudno and Great Yarmouth. It was mainly because of these services that SUT approached the Abbey Lane business with a view to a takeover. After the war, Abbey Lane Motors never regained their pre-war position

and as a result, a very dilapidated fleet was in use. On the 20th May 1953, SUT assumed control of this company, but only a few of the acquired vehicles entered SUT stock and even those that did, did not remain for much longer than a year. Perhaps one of the most lucrative services was that to Great Yarmouth which had been acquired with the takeover of Abbey Lane Motor Services mentioned above, which in turn had acquired this service after the acquisition of SB Hogg. Travel habits change and although more people bought their own cars and consequently fewer people travelled by coach, coaching still had a role to play. Excursions formed a very important part in the company's portfolio, with many destinations featured. Some were repeated annually, whilst others operated for just one or two seasons. Half day, full day and evening trips were popular; perhaps one of the most popular being to Blackpool Illuminations, with both full and half day excursions offered. Just before the 'National' era, it was common to offer about 100 different excursions to places of interest each year. Although most of the fleet was de-licensed for the winter it was more than made up for during the high season when the hiring in of vehicles for excursions would more than double the entire fleet strength.

It must be remembered that in the years just after the war, the couriers or 'conductors' as they

Above: An immaculate looking AEC Regal in the fleet of Abbey Lane Motor Services (Beauchief Coaches) in the duo green/yellow livery adopted by this concern. **AWJ 722** had a Burlingham body. Incidentally, the name Beauchief Coaches was chosen after the area of Sheffield in which it was based. (*STA*)

Below: **AWJ 722** again, but after it had been rebuilt by Abbey Lane Motors themselves, using much of the original framework and re-positioning the entrance. Seen on the forecourt at Charlotte Road after acquisition and repainted briefly into SUT livery, it has been given fleet number **106**. The photograph was taken in October 1954, shortly before withdrawal. (*Tom Robinson*)

Another former Beauchief Coaches vehicle was **CWA 348**, an AEC Regal 0662, again with a body built by Abbey Lane Motor Services themselves and looking a little neater than No. 106. The original body was by Cravens when new in 1936 whilst the one illustrated was constructed in 1946. It was numbered **108** in SUT stock. (*Tom Robinson*)

were known then, were very much pioneers especially in long haul Continental travel. There were no motorways then, signposting was primitive, the volume of traffic was much less, in many instances these men had to find their own way about. Although a basic itinerary was produced and maps supplied, to a great extent these would be less than useful especially after the ravages of war in many of the countries encountered. It was up to the individual driver, therefore, as to how much effort they put in and consequently how successful was the tour.

The General Manager, Benjamin Goodfellow, arrived at SUT in 1948 as Assistant General Manager, becoming General Manager the following year. He was undoubtedly a most innovative and flamboyant character and it was he and his Chief Engineer Ronald Burgin (who later became General Manager, and who commenced his career at County Motors of Lepton) who put SUT firmly on the map. Ben Goodfellow had arrived at SUT from North Western, where he had been Assistant Engineer

since 1933, following the takeover of his family's business by North Western in December 1932.

During the 1950s and 1960s all tours, both in this country and abroad, were operated by SUT's own vehicles. Some went overseas with their passengers, while other coaches were stationed abroad for the duration of the season. A notable exception to this was in the early 1950s, when such was the demand for the tours, that coaches were hired from Blue Cars, Red Line Continental and Timpsons. Unusual tours included a 'Radio Luxembourg' tour during 1953 where passengers could go on-air to record a message for family and friends at home. This nine-day tour cost £29 18s 6d (£29.92½). The same year a 'Coronation' tour was announced which was for seven days featuring sightseeing around London and Windsor for £26 16s 6d (£26.82½). In 1959 the company was the first British operator to send a coach into Morocco. The tour again was a success but, however, the heat managed to buckle roof panels on the coach. Holiday tours in England, Scotland and Wales all featured prominently as did tours to Eire and

Jersey. Another innovation was a tour to Yugoslavia, introduced in the 1960s.

On 13th November 1956, Ben Goodfellow received a request from Mr Petty, a London businessman, who was sponsoring coaches to take part in a relief mission for Hungary. SUT was chosen at the suggestion of Mr RV Black of AEC. Immediately Messrs Goodfellow and Burgin agreed to get the ball rolling. The first coach selected was a new Burlingham-bodied Reliance, VWE 258 'Copenhagen' and it was ready in two hours. George Bassett, the sweet manufacturer, donated 20 bags of sugar weighing approximately one ton. Dixon Pitchfork sent toffee, whilst the Sheffield WVS and Civil Defence sent food and clothing. Esso supplied the fuel and an extra 50 sealed diesel canisters were carried. Tyre mileage was underwritten by Goodyear. The coach arrived in Vienna 36 hours after leaving Sheffield. Returning to Sheffield, the coach brought refugees back to this country. A further six trips were made by SUT, each of two expeditions in three coaches. Drivers involved were Norman Robertson, Bert Oxley, Marcel (Matt) Mattison, Ken Warrilow and Rafe Byron-Thompson using coaches TWJ 249 'Hatton', TWJ 252 'Gilbert' (both Duple bodied Reliances) VWE 259 'Amsterdam' and VWE 261 'Montreux' (both Reliances with Burlingham bodies). Altogether over 250 refugees were evacuated to Britain. Mr Goodfellow made this statement to the local press: – "A little aid at once is worth a million promises – Sheffield is leading the way in this practical type of relief work."

SUT continued to purchase various other independents, Gladys Hibberd of City Road coming under their wing in June 1957. Another Derbyshire company taken over on the 1st July 1958 was William Edwin Pashley of Bradwell, where the small garage here was retained for many years as an outstation. When Pashley's was taken over, the vehicles involved in the sale were really surplus to requirements and did not fit in with the vehicle policy at Charlotte Road. It was eventually decided to convert a Duple Elizabethan-bodied Reliance so that the centre entrance door was operated by the driver! This was the only stage service operated by SUT which ran between Hope Station and Bradwell and necessitated the employment of a 'clippie' in the shape of Mrs M Thompson who lived in the village of Bradwell. The licence for the service soon passed to North

Western Road Car in the following year, although Brookside garage was retained by SUT until 1978.

Emmanuel Jeffcock of Balaclava Road, who specialized in fishing trips and named his coaches after fish (Bream, Pike, etc), was taken over in June 1959. Following on from this was George Ernest Whiteley of Langsett Road, on 1st November 1960. The penultimate takeover was that of John Walter Fantom of Duke Street and Queens Road, this being on 10th May 1963. Lastly, Hirst & Sweeting of Holme Lane completed SUT's takeovers on 15th March 1967. Here again the premises were retained. In addition to its tours, both British and Continental, the company also had very lucrative excursions, express, private hire and contract services. Incoming tourists to this country were also catered for, not least, for the round Britain tour, undertaken on behalf of Atlas Tours for parties of Australians in particular. The vehicles displayed their fleet name in lieu of the SUT logo. Private hire was another lucrative sphere in which the company operated. When the football World Cup was held in this country in 1966, one of the grounds chosen for some of the games was that of Sheffield Wednesday Football Club. It was SUT who had the job of transporting the various teams between hotels and venues, and supplying cars for the many dignitaries to the various locations. The cars, incidentally, were hired from dealers for this purpose. To quote an advertisement 'From 1 to 100 coaches for hire'. I do not think they ever managed to hire out the entire fleet but in 1963, when Prince Philip was to open a new Alloy Steel Plant for the English Steel Corporation at Tinsley Park, no fewer than 26 coaches were requested to transport VIPs, officials, employees and guests around the huge plant and to ferry them to waiting trains.

For a number of years, special duties were also performed. Demonstration vehicles were hired, for example, by Batchelors Peas Ltd as mobile soup kitchens which toured the country. Stephenson Blake, the stationers and printers, and Brooks Safety Belts had SUT coaches converted for their specific use. Frigidaire hired a Burlingham bodied Reliance of 1956 complete with a load of fridges (how they managed to get them on board was another matter!) and driver Jack Stone had the honour of driving around England with the manufacturer's representatives extolling the virtues of Frigidaire. Support vehicles were supplied for the Monte Carlo Rally from 1954 until the 1960s, using AEC Regal IVs with Windover Kingsway bodies. Joe Loss and His Orchestra had a contract with the company which lasted for seven years for the supply of an Orchestra coach. Similar transport was undertaken for Count Basie, The Platters, Eddie Condon and his Orchestra and even Laurel and Hardy, who were chauffeured in one of two Humber Pullmans owned during the early 1950s. The very first Windover Kingsway coach body built for the company in 1950 was numbered 197 (MWJ 197) and classed in what was to become the 'Gay' series. This particular machine was called 'Gay Discovery'. These vehicles were named after Gaynor Goodfellow, the daughter of the General Manager.

In 1957 Ben Goodfellow, the General Manager, and his right had man Ron Burgin, Chief Engineer, approached Burlingham with a design for a large windowed coach with a view to introducing this type into the fleet. This company was chosen as they were currently supplying vehicles to the SUT. However, Burlingham were less than enthusiastic about the idea and said the design was not feasible and would not have widespread appeal, being too futuristic. Undaunted, Ben and Ron next approached Plaxton, partly due to the fact that they had been more than impressed with the build quality of the two vehicles that were ex Altrincham Coachways, particularly since one had been involved in an accident, the results of which were minimal to the structure. Plaxton's were more than happy to oblige and work began on designing a large-window coach based around their current Venturer and Consort products. The following year the Panorama was born. As a matter of interest, the name 'Panorama' was suggested by John Otter, an electrician at SUT who won a competition organized by Ben Goodfellow to put forward a name for the new class of coach. He won £5 for his effort – not bad considering this was 1958! The first design was a batch of six that was unique to the company, the last two of which had a slightly revised side trim and in the process looked even better than the previous four, being more in keeping with the body lines.

The Plaxton Panorama body, designed by the Goodfellow/Burgin team, together with Plaxton's of Scarborough, entered the fleet during 1958. Various design changes took place with the Panorama in ensuing years and perhaps the most noticeable step forward came when new legislation allowed the use of 36-foot long single-deck vehicles. SUT was first off the mark with the launch of its No. 326, appropriately enough registered 136 AWJ. This was an AEC Reliance AH470-engined machine with a lengthened body to the new dimensions. It was launched by the Lord Mayor of Sheffield, Alderman JW Sterland, on 10th October 1961.

Ben Goodfellow had observed very early on the advantages of entering his coaches in both National and International Coach Rallies. Indeed,

If you've earned it, show if off! Ron Burgin, Chief Engineer (left) and Ben Goodfellow, General Manager, admire the many awards attributed to No. **318** (**1318 WA**) which it had accumulated at the Nice International, the British Coach Rally at Brighton and the National Rally at Blackpool in 1961. The coach had been rebuilt following a horrific crash at Huntingdon, Cambridgeshire on Boxing Day 1960 with the Sheffield Wednesday football team on board. (*SUT*)

the first event of this kind which was held in Montreux in 1949 was attended by an SUT coach. For many years after, both this rally, one at Nice and indeed the first British Coach Rally at Clacton in 1955, saw the company participating. Indeed, they also entered the first National Coach Rally held in Blackpool in 1961. Many awards have been made to SUT from all these events through the years but upon the retirement of Ben Goodfellow, the entering of vehicles in such rallies ceased, at least until National took over. The company stayed loyal to Plaxton for all its new vehicles from 1958 (with the exception of one Burlingham product delivered in 1960) until a change in policy during the early 1970s. Legislation which led to the formation of the National Bus Company (NBC) resulted in all former BET and Transport Holding Company fleets becoming part of the NBC. As part of the BET group, SUT subsequently became a unit of the NBC in January 1969.

From its inception, a largely Leyland and AEC fleet had been inherited from the various constituents and to a lesser extent Morris, Karrier and Dennis. Bodywork featured such names as Eastwood & Kenning, Reeve & Kenning,

Burlingham, Duple, Bellhouse Hartwell, Windover and of course Plaxton. However, early on in the company's existence, advantage was taken to market the value of locally built Cravens products, a fact which had previously been exploited by the various constituents. Vehicle purchasing policy continued to favour AEC and this remained so until the demise of the company. Sadly, the last Plaxton-bodied coaches entered the fleet during 1972; incidentally, these were the last machines in the familiar red and grey livery. From the following year, although the AEC was still favoured, it was decided by the powers that be to have the newly introduced Dominant body from Duple mounted to these. Sure enough, the years 1973 and 1974 saw this combination of vehicle purchased and were duly delivered in the 'all over' white scheme adopted for the coach liveries of NBC, although, as if by token gesture, both years' coaches had the legend 'Sheffield United Tours' in red over the front wheel arches. This gave way on new vehicles delivered in 1975 to the title 'North East'; eventually this was abbreviated to just 'East'.

Harry 'Nippy' Norman stands proudly in front of No. **322 (1322 WA)** whilst on the Bournemouth, Isle of Wight and Folkestone tour in the early 1960s. Upon withdrawal in 1973 it was sold to a Chesterfield school. This particular coach was stored at the Sheffield Bus Museum, old Tinsley Tram Sheds in Sheffield, and is now at the South Yorkshire Bus Museum, Aldwarke, Rotherham, pending restoration.

The Human Element

The unsung heroes of a company are those that rarely, if ever, come into direct contact with the travelling public. Traffic management, schedules, tours charting, mechanics, painters, electricians, coach trimmers, cleaners, the list goes on. In general, the days of SUT were pre-computerisation and as such were more reliant on the human element, at least as far as clerical jobs were concerned, for the smooth running of the company. Perhaps it was for the better as a more personal approach was possible. The driver and/or courier was generally the immediate individual with whom passengers would come into contact; therefore it was essential that he was capable of good PR work. I say 'he' as no female drivers were employed. Uniforms were another aspect where a smartly turned out driver could really 'sell' the company. In the case of SUT, their uniform was one of a black blazer, grey trousers, a monogrammed tie and a breast pocket badge. It was not left up to the individual to wear what they liked, neither were they issued with a full uniform including a hat, which to my mind would have

made it appear too starchy – more like a bus driver. The blazer/trouser approach was smart yet casual, more in keeping with the leisure industry. However, prior to this, smart white dust coats had been provided, initially with UMS in white letters on a red collar to be replaced after the war with SUT lettering. In the early 1950s, a brown gabardine suit had been issued, which to say the least, was less than smart. In this guise, drivers were referred to as 'Bennie's Brown Boys' (Ben Goodfellow was at that time General Manager).

Some drivers were very much in the public eye and featured heavily in local and trade press. Dick Midgley was a tours driver but also selected by the company to enter in International Coach Rallies. Indeed, the first such rally held after the war was in Montreux in 1949. Dick, together with his courier John L Edwards, entered their AEC Regal/Windover for the event and came away with first prize. This success was repeated the following year, again with Dick at the wheel. More rallies followed, not only in Montreux but also at Nice. Nearer to home, both the British Coach Rally held initially at Clacton, and subsequently at Brighton and the National Coach Rally in Blackpool were

Somewhere in the West Country Joe Moffatt is seen with his steed No. **329** (**329 BWB**). This batch of 2U3RA coaches came in a different colour from the rest of the fleet. This was not so much noticeable when viewed on their own but when seen alongside other coaches it was obviously more an eau-de-nil green/grey; a fact backed by foreman painter Ray Birkett.

to see SUT take part. Other drivers returning to Sheffield with an assortment of silverware were Jack Hancock, Arnie Wilson, Bert Carr, Harry (Nippy) Norman and Matt Mattison. Such rallies were a platform for coach companies to show off their latest purchases and gain much publicity in doing so.

Two drivers were awarded the BEM for their devotion to their jobs. George Hill was awarded his in 1972, whilst Frank Carr received his in 1980. Frank had over 50 years unbroken service starting with AF Hancock, through to SUT and right into the National era.

A somewhat unenviable task undertaken on an annual basis, usually by Jack Hancock and Freddie Couldstone, was that of collecting new chassis from the AEC factory in Southall, West London and driving them to Charlotte Road. When the time came for the body to be fitted, they were then taken on again, usually to either HV Burlingham in Blackpool or Plaxton's in Scarborough. Bear in mind this was usually carried out in winter, open to the elements and all you had in the way of comfort was a wooden seat. The only advantage was that in the absence of bodywork "you couldn't half motor!"

Each year a Reunion Ball was held for patrons of the company together with staff and guests at the City Hall in Sheffield and each year a different theme was employed. In 1959, for example, there was a Dutch theme, and miniature windmills were placed around the room, all having been made in the company's workshop. Maids in pretty Dutch outfits served food from a menu inspired by Dutch cuisine. An organ specifically obtained for the occasion was also shipped in! Stars of stage and radio would put in appearances with such names as Max Bygraves, Joe Loss and Reginald Dixon entertaining the guests. Sheffield Transport even provided special trams for the event!

Keith Houghton, Assistant Chief Engineer at SUT from the mid 1960s, tells of an instance where a coach was being reversed off the side park at the garage, assisted by an employee, who realised afterwards that the coach was being stolen. Eventually, it turned up in a farmer's field in Lincolnshire where it sustained more damage being extricated than it received driving it there in the first place. Ron Hailes, a driver who started work at the company just after the war and who sadly died whilst I was preparing this book, recounted to me how difficult it was in those early

Seen taking a comfort stop whilst on tour is No. **375** (**KWE 375D**) with courier George Hill assisting a passenger to alight. The other courier on this tour, seen standing in the cab area is Frank Carr, who started his career with AF Hancock. As mentioned in the text above, both these employees received the British Empire Medal for their services to coaching. (*STA*)

post war years. He told me of instances where he would return from a trip quite often in the early hours of the morning, go home if possible, have literally a couple of hours sleep, before returning to the garage to do his next stint behind the wheel.

It was generally acknowledged that the fleet was kept in immaculate condition despite the fact many coaches were stored outdoors throughout the winter. This was due in no small way to the efforts of bodymen, trimmers, painters etc. Ray Birkett was in the latter position from leaving school around 1948 and with the exception of two years absence for National Service, served his entire career with the company and its successor,

National. Every single vehicle was brush painted and the finish obtained by Ray and his colleagues had to be seen to be believed. People like Ray were the rule rather than the exception at SUT. Many employees had wives, husbands, sons and daughters working alongside each other. When the company came under the National banner, much of the atmosphere, friendliness and individuality was unfortunately lost. In many travellers' eyes, National was too large and impersonal and this was reflected in the drop of patronage. National though, is another story and I do not intend to cover this aspect, but will leave that to others.

On a lovely day in Derbyshire just past a local beauty spot known as Toads Mouth, on return to Sheffield is No. **408** (**DWA 408H**) while on a test run with Assistant Chief Engineer Keith Houghton at the wheel.(*SUT*)

SUT Story –
Personal Recollections

I have, as far as I can remember, always been interested in buses and coaches with a definite bias toward the latter. In Sheffield, the distinctive red and grey of SUT stood out from the blue and cream of the corporation vehicles, both looking very smart despite being based in what was a very grimy industrial city in the early 1950s. My initial recollections of half-cab Regal 1s and 111s with Duple and Windover bodies were founded on evening trips into Derbyshire with my parents. These trips were the highlight of the year, indeed they were our only trips as they were classed as our holidays, not being able to afford a week's holiday at a seaside resort. It must be said that these outings were very popular with the Sheffield public, and many 'hired in' coaches were also employed on exotic runs to places such as Buxton, Castleton, Calver, Eyam, Bakewell and Monsal Dale to name but a few. Around 1953/4 we started taking our annual holiday of one week in Blackpool. My earliest recollections of travel to this resort were by AEC Regals with Windover Huntingdon bodies. Arrival at the Coliseum Coach Station opened up a whole new horizon for me. I remember sitting on a full front AEC Regal III with Windover body at the Coliseum for our return to Sheffield. These particular machines were very handsome and comfortable too. A pre-selective gearbox; the deep cushioned moquette-covered seats; the solid clunk of the sliding entrance door being closed and the sight of those huge Clayton bulkhead heaters which were, to say the least, rather hot especially when any idiot, self included, put their hands on them. Interior pillar-mounted saloon lights which dimmed when the vehicle started up and the distinctive smell of Zoflora which greeted you, are the things of nostalgia which cannot be replicated artificially.

A more asserted effort towards my enthusiasm for the company came sometime around 1956 with my first of many visits to the Charlotte Road garage of SUT. I had been train spotting at the Midland Station with my father, witnessing the arrival of the 'Thames Clyde Express', and after downing a ham roll and a bottle of lemonade, was asked if I wanted to go to a coach depot? – Did I! After what seemed a very long walk, we finally arrived and the sight that greeted us was

unbelievable. Stacked inside the garage were Windover Kingsway bodied AEC Regal IVs, which seemed massive. Newer Reliances with Duple bodies of the Elizabethan variety delivered 1954/5 were also on view. Although by no means my favourite vehicles in the fleet, they were nevertheless, impressive. A couple of coaches which certainly left favourable impressions were the then recently delivered Burlingham Seagull-bodied Reliances. Everything about these seemed just right and the livery suited them well. In the 'graveyard' beside the garage were older but none the less very smart Windover Huntingdon bodied Regal IIIs with both half-cab and fully fronted bodywork. From my first ever visit I was treated very favourably by everyone at SUT, including office staff, drivers, maintenance staff and management, which continued throughout my many visits there. The company was very innovative and was the first to place a Windover Kingsway in service. It was also the first to introduce the Panorama and the first company in Great Britain to place a 36 foot-long vehicle in service on the 10th October 1961, as mentioned previously. I have had the pleasure over the years of availing myself of their transport on tours (only British I may add), excursions, express, private hire and even contract work.

On a couple of occasions in the 1950s, I even travelled on a Regal/Windover working on a bus service on hire to Sheffield Transport, using an honesty box mounted on the front bulkhead into which you placed your fare. Many times I have travelled to Great Yarmouth, usually on a Windover Kingsway Regal IV or a Duple Elizabethan-bodied Reliance. Initially, the loading and unloading point was on Albemarle Road in that town. When a coach arrived with its load of holiday makers, the returning passengers would literally wave and cheer at the sight of the SUT coaches pulling into view. It was very impressive seeing perhaps 15 or more vehicles all in red and grey lined up there. Later years saw the loading point moved to the old disused railway station – not quite the same. In the early 1950s, shortly after Windover Kingsways had been introduced on Continental tours, a problem arose whereby one such vehicle was ready to be 'lifted' on board the ferry when the crane operative noticed the vehicle was overweight. It must be remembered here that this was before roll-on, roll-off ferries and that an unloaded Kingsway weighed in the region of 9½ tons. After phone calls to Sheffield, it was agreed that on this occasion the coach would be allowed to sail, on condition that no more overweight vehicles be dispatched on such duties. However, Mr Goodfellow ordered that future vehicles used should have their unladen written weight reduced by 1½ tons. Yes this did happen and yes it worked!

Over the years, hundreds, in fact thousands, of hired-in coaches have appeared on excursions. Some were very smart machines whilst a few others gave the general impression that they were somewhat overdue at a Barnsley scrap yard. Two vehicles I remember well, although never travelled on either, were the Bellhouse Hartwell Landmaster-bodied Reliances TWJ 253/4. These were amongst the last such bodies built by this Westhoughton-based bodybuilder and I believe originally ordered by Blue Cars for mounting onto Leyland chassis. The floors on both machines had to be rebuilt very early on in their lives and the outward hinged entrance doors also proved to be a problem. Despite this I liked both in a strange sort of way.

One vehicle I never travelled on was number 333 (333 BWB), which was the sole Leyland Leopard. I never liked this much as it had a lower driving position, an antiquated dash panel with square instruments and it did not sound the same as a Reliance. Neither did it like hills apparently. I was not the only one who did not like it, as most of the drivers thought the same. Perhaps one of the reasons for this might have been that they were 'weaned' on AECs, so why should you have to have margarine when you could have butter? Mention should be made of one of Ben Goodfellow's prize possessions. This was 336 DWJ, known as 'Show Boat' or 'Bennie's Pride'. Based on the usual AEC Reliance/Plaxton Panorama combination, 336 was exhibited on the Plaxton stand at the Earls Court Motor Show in 1962. Instead of the usual chrome side strips, so much a trademark of SUT coaches since 1950, it sported imitation wooden side panels in Arborite material which was laminated directly onto the metal panels. When new this machine was very impressive, sporting twin air-horns, drinks servery, drinks tables on seat backs and refrigerated air conditioning for use in hot climates. I must admit though that in later years, the Arborite tended to look more tired than the metal strips would have done. Unfortunately, this vehicle was written off in the early 1970s. Sadly for me SUT lost its identity in 1974 but, my memories remain, together with thousands of photographs and other memorabilia.

Acknowledgements

It is impossible to thank everyone individually who had helped me over the years in various ways to further my interest of Sheffield United Tours. But to all – I thank you. I would like to thank Peter Elliott, a good friend who persuaded me to write on the subject of SUT. Also my thanks to Paul Fox who has been a great help over the years and again a good friend. Thanks too to Tom and Patricia Robinson for the loan of a number of photographs and for the scanning of all the pictorial content, without whom this project would never have left the ground. Most of the photographs are from my own collection built up over many years; those that are not are acknowledged individually by each picture. Many thanks also to Keith Houghton, Dave Hancock and Ray Birkett for verifying many details and their knowledge of behind the scenes activities. Last but definitely not least my wonderful wife Julie and son Matthew who have put up with my constant mumblings during preparation of this book and for all the help and encouragement they have both given me, not to mention all the typing that has been done.

Trev Weckert
Sheffield
October 2006

The last brochure produced by the company for Continental tours pre-war. It featured holidays to the French Riviera, Switzerland and Paris in 1939.

Above: The first new coaches were ordered by the company during 1935. Six AEC Rangers fitted with Cravens 26-seat bodies. This official photograph of No. **32** (**AWJ 232**) was the first of the order. (*Cravens*)

Below: This postcard was used for advertising during the 1930s. Clearly displaying the 'United Motor Services' title on its rear end is No. **92** (**BWJ 603**). It was one of a batch of seven AEC Regal 662 with the stepped waist-rail Burlingham body new in 1936. These particular machines were the subject of a complicated body replacement exercise in 1950. (*SUT*)

Above: With East Dene, the house depicted in the background which for a number of years was the company's canteen and social club, and previously owned by the Caudle family, we see **BWJ 606**, an AEC Regal with the new Burlingham body it received in 1947. The vehicle itself was new in April 1936 and numbered **95**. It was withdrawn after the summer season in 1954. (*JH Turner*)

Below: The old Kitson garage at Pond Hill is the setting for this photo with one of the driver's wives, Mrs Frank Carr, leaning against the front wing. New in May 1937, **DWA 990** was one of a batch of four Leyland Cub KPZ2s with Burlingham coachwork seating 26 in its front entrance body and is seen here in 1938. All four were requisitioned by the Ministry of Supply (War) in 1940 and were returned to SUT by May 1943. (*F Carr*)

Above: The annual outing by Viners Limited, a well known Sheffield cutlery company, required a number of vehicles for the run to the coast. On this occasion, No. **103** (**DWA 992**), a Regal II with Burlingham 32-seat body and new in June 1937, is seen parked up on Marine Drive in Scarborough on what appears to be a rather wet day. This coach, along with six others from the batch of eight, were converted to Regal I specification by AEC during 1942. The complete batch was 103-10 (DWA 992-9), but these were not registered consecutively. (*WJ Haynes*)

Below: Not what it appears at first glance! Number **104** (**DWA 997**) was originally one of the eight Regal IIs purchased in 1937. Of this batch, No. 105 (DWA 994), was requisitioned by the Admiralty and re-registered 597 RN during 1941. The remainder, No. **104** included, were converted to diesel in 1942.

Above: Exhibited at the Scottish Commercial Motor Show in 1938 this Regal/Burlingham combination was to remain unique in the fleet. Seen here displaying incorrect registration of **DWA 999**, it was in fact licensed as **EWE 468** becoming No. **111** in the fleet. It was converted to oil engine in November 1946 and then converted to towing duties for SUT during 1951. (*HV Burlingham*)

Below: The same vehicle after conversion to towing vehicle seen in the side yard at Charlotte Road. It was never repainted and was finally withdrawn for scrap in 1957. (*Tom Robinson*)

Above: In June 1934 Hancock's took delivery of **AWA 331**, a Leyland Lion LT5A which had a locally built Cravens rear entrance body mounted to it. However, due to body deterioration SUT decided to have it re-bodied by Duple in 1939 and is seen here numbered **S62**. The rear end was painted red, a feature that was phased out, as was the UMS lettering, when Ben Goodfellow became General Manager. (*STA*)

Below: Another former Hancock's coach to receive a new body during 1939 was **S50** (**AWA 334**) but this time the chassis was a Leyland Tiger TS6. Originally with Cravens bodywork (as was sister coach AWA 333, which was rebodied at the same time), this was one of the vehicles that spent some time with Crosville during World War 2. Note that the door slides inside the body. (*STA*)

Above: This Leyland Cub KPZ4 was bodied by Duple from new in 1939. As far as I know the only other fleet to purchase this combination was the Plymouth Co-operative Society but whereas the latter had sliding entrance doors, the SUT examples had outward hinged ones. No.**S85** (**FWJ 775**) received Hancock's Motor Tours lettering. (*STA*)

Below: An interior view of **S85** shows mirrored bulkhead, pillar mountings, saloon lamps and ornamental curtains. Interior fittings were mainly finished in burgundy, beige and light brown materials. What opulence! (*STA*)

Above: The smart uncluttered lines of the Duple body are seen to good advantage on No. **S80** (**FWJ 770**) a Leyland Tiger TS8 of 1939. This design pre-dates the later 'A' type body of which SUT had over twenty. The ribbon over the fleet name proclaims United Motor Services.

Below: A very dismal day for a fleet of coaches about to depart from Castlegate in Sheffield sometime in 1939. The leading coach is No. **81** (**FWJ 771**), which was the newest and was delivered that year and was one of five Leyland Tiger TS8s with handsome Duple 32-seat bodies. The original engines were replaced by Leyland E181 7.4 litre diesel units in June 1947. Unfortunately, the destination is not known.

Above: One of the 25 coaches delivered during 1946-48 and photographed in Leeds is **HWJ 980** (fleet number **127**) a Duple 'A' type bodied AEC Regal I 0662. Surplus vehicles in this batch were eagerly snapped up by both East Yorkshire Motor Services and Yorkshire Traction. (*WJ Haynes*)

Below: By far the largest single batch of vehicles delivered to the company were 25 AEC Regal 0662s with Duple 'A' bodies, numbered 116-40 (HWJ 969-93), delivery commencing in 1946. Here representing the batch is No. **138** (**HWJ 991**), seen looking slightly weary in front of the garage. (*Tom Robinson*)

Opposite page: What is now referred to as a comfort stop is being taken by **S172** (**KWA 712**), a classic AEC Regal III with Windover Huntingdon coachwork. It was undertaking the Lands End tour around 1950. A number of this particular batch received unofficial names as in this case 'Highland Monarch'. (*J Higham collection*)

Above: Taking a break at the top of Porlock Hill in Somerset is No. **143** (**JWE 636**), whilst on an Ilfracombe and Bournemouth tour in 1948. This was one of the first Windover Huntingdon bodied AEC Regal I 0662 to enter the fleet, in 1948. The batch totalled twelve, Nos. 141-52 (JWE 634-45) and they were far more luxurious than their Duple counterparts. This vehicle was one of eight exported to Yugoslavia in 1954 entering service with GSP, Belgrade. (*F Carr*)

Below: Originally ordered by South Wales Transport, Nos. 175-8 (KWA 715-8) were diverted to SUT in 1949 but had to have drop frame chassis extensions fitted by the bodybuilder, Windover, before being bodied to their Huntingdon design. The chassis were Regal III 6821A type. Alongside No. **178** is No. **174** (**KWA 714**), a similar vehicle but ordered directly by SUT. (*Tom Robinson*)

Above: Former coach **166** (**KWA 706**), an AEC Regal III 0682 with Windover Huntingdon coachwork, was converted to towing duties during May 1957, it having been new in 1949. It is seen at Calver Sough on 8th August 1960 collecting tram seats from Sheffield tram 133, which had been found in a garden. Employees had borrowed 166 to transport the tram seats for use on a preserved tram, number 46, which is now at Crich. The 'Red Herring' as it was known, due to its all over red livery, was finally withdrawn in 1970. (*Tom Robinson*)

Below: Cautiously proceeding over the New Bridge over the River Dart is Harry 'Nippy' Norman taking **179** (**KWA 719**), on a Torquay tour in 1950. This AEC Regal III 0962 had Windover Huntingdon coachwork and also carried an unofficial name plaque on the bonnet side, which was removed before return to depot. In this instance it was 'Devonian'. The General Manager did not approve of "unofficial" naming of coaches unless it was his idea!

Above: Here is No. **186** (**LWE 886**) previously withdrawn from service during 1958 but now back at Charlotte Road after being 'hired back' to cover a vehicle shortage from July to September 1959. It is a full fronted AEC Regal III 682IA with Windover Huntingdon coachwork. (*Tom Robinson*)

Below: At rest in the garage yard we see No. **195** (**LWE 895**), another of the full-fronted eight-feet wide Regal/ Windover Huntingdons. The circular kerb window was an unofficial modification carried only by this vehicle, having been fitted by its regular driver Gilbert Howsham. The conversion was very much frowned upon by management. (*Tom Robinson*)

On Chelsea Bridge, London bound for Montreux in Switzerland and the second International Coach Rally there in 1950, is No. **192** (**LWE 892**). This batch, numbered 191-6, were the first 8-feet wide vehicles in the fleet and as such were restricted for a while as to which services they could operate. The AEC Regal 9621E chassis had a Windover Huntingdon body and was the outright winner! (*Windover*)

The prototype Windover Kingsway body was introduced on an AEC Regal IV with pre-selector gearbox which went into service as No.**197** (**MWJ 197**) in 1950. It was exhibited at the Earls Court Motor Show that year and sported reclining seats, cocktail bar, curtains and a rear lounge. It was also the first coach whose registration mark matched the fleet number. The destination indicators were short lived and were soon replaced by dome windows. (*SUT*)

Above: Three Windover Kingsway Regal IV are seen here on a private function. This class of coach became known as the 'Gay' class, following the naming of them after the then General Manager's daughter, Gaynor Goodfellow. Nearest the camera is **NWB 200** 'Gay Cutler', to its left is **NWB 203** 'Gay Cavalier' whilst the third vehicle is unidentifiable.

Below: In all, no fewer than 32 Kingsways entered service with SUT. All but six had pre-selective gear boxes. **OWA 214** was one of those which had synchromesh gearboxes. Later 'christened' Gay Montreux it had a rear entrance and toilet fitted.

Above: Far from its old hunting grounds is No. **215** (**OWB 215**), a pre-selective AEC Regal IV in service with Transportes Melenara, Gran Canaria to whom it was sold in June 1960. Its Windover Kingsway body was by now converted to right hand side loading and had been re-registered **GC-15136** by its new owner and given fleet number **8**. (*Tom Robinson*)

Below: Norman Robertson is seen taking instructions from an AA patrolman in this publicity shot taken during the 1955 Monte Carlo Rally. **PWB 222** 'Gay Consort' was the support coach for the British entrants.

BY APPOINTMENT TO
H.M. THE KING
COACH BUILDERS

WINDOVERS LTD

Montreux Premier award 1949-1950

The new Windover coach, specially designed for continental touring, will be operated by Sheffield United Tours Ltd., who in 1949 and 1950 won premier award at Montreux with a Windover body mounted on A.E.C. chassis.

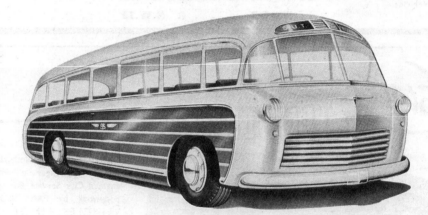

Composite wood and steel construction, aluminium panelling, mounted on A.E.C. "Regal" Mk. IV underfloor engine chassis, 31 seats. Fully enclosed front, central entrance, twin sliding perspex-panelled roofs, full-drop safety-glass windows. Interior heating and ventilating system, with separate heating for rear of saloon. Automatic folding step to offside emergency door. Ample rear luggage locker.

Coachwork specialists since 1796

THE HYDE, HENDON, LONDON, N.W.9   *Telephone : Colindale 4031-2-3-4*

It was perhaps inevitable that once AEC commenced supplying SUT with its Regal IV chassis Windovers would want to use one of the company's new Kingsway bodies in advertisements. This artist's impression of one appeared in the October/November 1950 issue of *Bus and Coach*. The June 1951 issue incorporated a photograph rather than this drawing. (*STA*)

Not quite what it appears to be! Seen here in Rome travelling the wrong way through an archway due to flood diversion is **LUW 454**, an AEC Regal IV with Windover Kingsway coachwork - complete with SUT shield below the windscreen and SUT lettering in its destination box, this Timpson coach was being driven by Norman Robertson.

Above: The penultimate Kingsway entered service in 1954 as **RWE 227**. Seen whilst operating the Great Yarmouth service it is believed to be parked on Albemarle Road in the years before conversion of the railway station into a coach park. It was withdrawn in 1961.

Below: During February 1954 two AEC Regal IVs with Plaxton Venturer bodies became surplus to requirements with their owners Altrincham Coachways. The vehicles, RMB 158 and JBU 164 were purchased by SUT and given numbers 229 and 230 respectively. Only a few months old when they came to Sheffield, both were in their previous owner's livery of blue and cream and entered service as that with SUT. Shortly afterwards, the blue panels were repainted red whilst the cream was retained for a while before giving way to full SUT livery. Parked outside Charlotte Road without metal side fleet names is No. **229**. (*Tom Robinson*)

Above: In 1953 Duple announced a new body design for underfloor engined vehicles to be called the Elizabethan. SUT decided to order 22 of the type to be mounted on the AEC Reliance MU3RV chassis for delivery in 1954/5. The very first to enter service in the fleet was No. **232** (**RWE 232**), named 'Raleigh', after Elizabethan heroes – it is seen at the Coliseum Coach Station in Blackpool.

Below: Parked up at Westwood in Scarborough is No. **238** (**SWA 238**), 'Marlowe', whilst on excursion duties with another SUT at the rear. It may be of interest to learn that this batch of Elizabethans (SWA233-42) entered service without metal fleet names, due to a dispute with the suppliers. Eventually this was resolved and each badge cost £ 11s 3d.

Above: Beauty is in the eye of the beholder. Not many seemed to like the Bellhouse Hartwell 'Landmaster' but as there were only two examples in the SUT fleet, numbers 253/4 (TWJ 253/4), they made quite a contrast to other AECs. The first of the duo is seen here on delivery day, 16th April 1955. It may be of interest to note that the body order was believed to be a cancelled one placed by Blue Cars for mounting onto Leyland chassis. Both vehicles were nicknamed Marilyn Monroes or The Twins for obvious reasons and the grill was that used on contemporary Standard Vanguard Phase II cars. (*Tom Robinson*)

Below: The first mini bus purchased by the company came in December 1956 and was used for feeder work and staff transport. **XWJ 985** was a VW Microbus painted from new in orange and chocolate brown livery. It never received SUT livery and neither did it sport any fleet names. I can never recall it displaying legal lettering either. (*SUT*)

Above: Leading vehicle here is No. **263** (**VWE 263**) whilst on the Yorkshire Coast Tour. The Burlingham Seagull bodied AEC Reliances in the fleet were known as the 'Continental Class' and as such this coach was named 'Vienna'. Various specifications featured on the first batch of 12 and a number, this vehicle included, featured air-conditioning by Key Leather Ltd as can be seen looking at the pod on the roof. (*Tom Robinson*)

Below: The Suez crisis in 1957 meant that a smaller British Coach Rally would be held that year and the venue was Battersea Park in London. The company decided to send two vehicles, so much for the fuel crisis! One was 265 (VWE 265) of the previous years' intake, whilst here we see No. **268** (**YWA 268**) 'Innsbruck'. This version of the Seagull known as the Mk V type featured a stowable seat headrest.

Above: Two specifications on the 1957 Seagulls meant that numbers 267-72 (YWA 267-72) had stowable headrests on the seats. Here No. **272** 'Cortina' shows most of the seats in the low back configuration whilst touring in Newquay. Incidently, this batch of vehicles was equipped with Webasto air conditioning units.

Below: The Burlingham Seagulls numbered 273-8 (YWA 273-8) had 41 seats known as the 'Oyster' type as depicted here on **273** 'Como' seen loading in Pond Street, Sheffield. Just visible in the nearside windscreen is the removable destination board which featured from new, made of Perspex with the destination embossed on it. (*RHG Simpson*)

Above: The final intake of Burlingham Seagulls arrived in 1958 and totalled six machines, all based on the usual Reliance MU3RV chassis. Representing this batch is **283** (**3283 WB**) 'Rome' seen rather appropriately at the Coliseum, but in Blackpool.

Below: Numerically the first Plaxton Panorama ever was No. **285** (**3285 WB**). The remainder of the six were numbers 286-90 (3286-90 WB) mounted on AEC Reliance MU3RV chassis. Appropriately named 'Panorama Pilot', it is seen leaving Wembley in the late 1950s. Upon withdrawal it went to Star Tours (Sheriff) of Gainsborough in 1968.

Above: The second Panorama produced was No. **286 (3286 WB),** aptly named 'Panorama Pioneer'. Here it is parked up ready to take part in the British Coach Rally of 1958 at Brighton. Driver Arnie Wilson took the vehicle to victory at this event and the famous rally driver of the time, Tommy Wisdom, assisted with the driving on the outward and return journeys. (*STA*)

Below: This series of Panoramas had their looks completely ruined with the fitment of two piece jack-knife doors during 1963-5. Illustrating the ugliness and lop-sided effect of this conversion is No. **287 (3287 WB)** which by then had lost its name 'Panorama Princess' in this view in the side yard at Charlotte Road.

Above: The last two machines in the 1958 intake of Panoramas had a slightly revised side trim whereby the top leading edge of the red side panels was straighter and ran parallel to the window line. Illustrating the point here is **289** (**3289 WB**) - 'Panorama Pilgrim' whilst on tour.

Below: During 1958 a redesign of the Panorama was undertaken and the following year the new type was added to stock. Based on the AEC Reliance 2MU3RV chassis, a batch of 12 numbered 291-6 (1291-6 WE) and 297-302 (6297-302 WE) went into service with variously 36, 40 and 41 seats featured. In this photo No. **291** 'Panorama Pride' is seen and was entered in the Geneva Show, the British Coach Rally at Brighton as well as being displayed at Earls Court. (*Plaxton*)

Above: The Yorkshire Coast Tour was being operated here by **292 (1292 WE)** 'Panorama Paramount' as coach number 3 in this view. Note how the air horns are still in evidence being fitted from new as result of this vehicle appearing at the Motor Show. This coach, in addition to appearing at the Motor Show, was also the Grand National coach. It was fitted with tables for BET/SUT hospitality use. (*STA*)

Below: A fine shot from the rear of No. **291** 'Panorama Pride' before being registered. Note the Venetian blinds, magazine nets and air horns. This coach was fitted with a prototype air conditioning unit from new, manufactured by Smith's Industries, adding a further £150 to the cost of the vehicle. Additionally, it was fitted with an Eberspacher turbo-charger, taking the output from the AH470 7.7-litre engine from 112 brake horse power to 140 brake horse power. (*STA*)

Above: Courier Jack Gosling in front of No. **294** (**1294 WE**) 'Panorama Paladin' whilst co-driver Arthur Stacey assists a passenger whilst on tour in Gibraltar in 1960.

Below: Driver Ashley Wall parades **299** (**6299 WE**) 'Panorama Progress' in a pageant whilst on a Newport and Isle of Wight tour during 1962. Bedecked in garlands, it was awarded third prize. The decorations were provided (unofficially) by the driver.

Above: 'Panorama Panache' was the name to grace **305** (**6305 WJ**) an AEC Reliance 2MU3RA with Plaxton Panorama 40-seat body which was new in 1960. Pictured here in Montreux it was eventually sold to Yorkshire Woollen in 1969. When new, it was used as the team coach for Sheffield Wednesday Football Club and was outright winner in at the 1960 British Coach Rally at Brighton, driven by Jack Hancock. It also went on to win the Nice International Rally the same year with Bert Carr at the wheel.

Below: Lined up with two more stable mates at Crich Tramway Museum whilst on the Crich and Matlock tour is **312** (**6312 WJ**), a 36 seat-tourer when new, but to my knowledge was one of the unnamed Panoramas.

Above: More associated with fishing trips was the fleet of Emanuel Jeffcock (Jeffs) who was taken over in June 1959. One of the coaches involved in the sale was **5827 WB**, a Bedford SB3 with Yeates Europa 41-seat coachwork seen in London carrying Jeffs red and green livery. Most coaches in this fleet received names of fish, this one being 'Bream'. It was given No. **J7** by its new owners.

Below: The solitary Thames Trader fitted with Plaxton Consort body arrived in 1960. The traditional SUT chrome strips were not carried by **313** (**3313 W**). Not too popular with SUT drivers either, it nevertheless stayed in the fleet for around seven years.

Above: Yet another oddity as regards bodywork was Thames Trader No. **314** (**3314 W**). This particular machine sported the newly introduced Seagull 60 body by Burlingham featuring a clerestory roof clearly visible in this view taken in London when new. Apparently, in some driver's eyes, this was a wonderful vehicle to drive! (*RF Mack*)

Below: Number **317** was one of a batch of three Thames Trader 570E models fitted with Plaxton Embassy 41-seat coachwork to enter the fleet in 1960. A further two similar machines entered service the following year. Seen at Waterdale in Doncaster having just been rammed from behind by another SUT vehicle, number **246** a Reliance/Duple Elizabethan. (*R Holmes*)

A view of No. **318 (1318 WA)** displaying the Panorama name on the front bumper at Scarborough, before delivery. This coach was the only one in the fleet to have a painted fleetname on the destination panel. The reason for this was that in place of destination equipment, a 45 rpm record player was installed from new. A drinks servery was installed at the rear. (*STA*)

Above: The very first 36-foot long coach in Britain was No. **326**, appropriately registered **136 AWJ** and was 'launched' by the Lord Mayor of Sheffield, Alderman JW Sterland on 10th October 1961. Here we see Norman Robertson piloting this 4MU3RA type Reliance in Boulogne whilst on tour. Unfortunately, this vehicle was converted to a stockcar transporter upon withdrawal in 1973.

Below: On its way to Blackpool for the Illuminations, driven by E Nolan, is No. **330** (**330 BWB**), which had been a successful entrant in the Nice International, Brighton and Blackpool coach rallies when new in 1962. This vehicle was also employed as one of the Sheffield Wednesday FC team coaches. An earlier coach employed on these duties (KWA 723) initially carried a football on the roof bearing the letters 'SWFC' when used for this purpose!

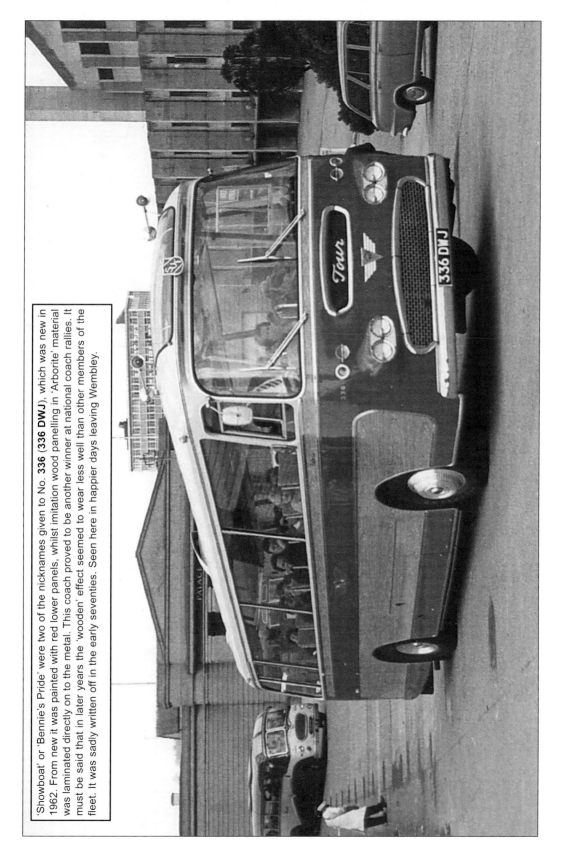

'Showboat' or 'Bennie's Pride' were two of the nicknames given to No. **336 (336 DWJ)**, which was new in 1962. From new it was painted with red lower panels, whilst imitation wood panelling in 'Arborite' material was laminated directly on to the metal. This coach proved to be another winner at national coach rallies. It must be said that in later years the 'wooden' effect seemed to wear less well than other members of the fleet. It was sadly written off in the early seventies. Seen here in happier days leaving Wembley.

Above: An oddity, which was not liked much by the drivers, was No. **333 (333 BWB)** the solitary Leyland Leopard PSU3/3R. A low driving position, poor acceleration, poor brakes and bad hill climbing ability being some of the reasons. It was, however, reliable. It is seen with Reliances parked alongside at the Coliseum in Blackpool.

Below: Again at the Coliseum, Blackpool we see No **341 (341 EWJ)**, an AEC Reliance, this time surrounded by various other SUT vehicles waiting to operate their tour of the Illuminations. Another of SUT's little quirks was the use of script lettering for destination screens for tours. However, as seen in this view, when undertaking Nation Express and Excursion duties, the destination was usually a paper sticker in the windscreen. (*RHG Simpson*)

Above: Another member of the 1963 batch seen here on Charlotte Road forecourt is No. **343** (**343 EWJ**), now a 48-seater. Devoid of fleet names and chrome strips on the red panels, this decision had been taken by the then Chairman, Frank Pointon, with a view to modernising appearances. This did nothing to improve individuality and the previous good looks of these fine machines. (*P Hanwell*)

Below: Whilst touring Torquay, No. **349** (**AWA 349B**) of 1964 is seen taking a break and displaying its low-backed touring seats. The scoop in the front bumper was an attempt by SUT to overcome overheating problems, but was not very successful. It did, however, create a loud 'drumming' noise inside the vehicle when at speed. Eventually this experiment was removed.

With the Forth Bridge as a backdrop, driver Jack Bateman halts No. **361** (**EWJ 361C**) whilst on tour during 1969. This 45-seater was one of ten new in 1965 with the revamped Panorama body, featuring the new front grille.

Above: Displaying the Bournemouth and Torquay tour blind when quite new is No. **363** (**EWJ 363C**) of 1965. Note how the front portion of the roof was painted red; this was soon repainted normal grey. (*M Jones*)

Below: On completion of the overseas portion of a Continental tour is No **367** (**KWE 367D**) in the blue and grey livery, disembarking the ferry at Dover and being driven by Cyril Everett. It will be noted the off-side portion of the windscreen is missing due to damage on tour. (*AEC*)

Number **375 (KWA 375D)** an AEC Reliance 2U3RA with 45-seater Plaxton Panorama body was used for number of publicity shots, as in this view. (STA)

Above: At speed whilst taking a party of tourists to Cattolica are drivers Frank Carr and George Hill, previously seen together on page 14. Again, the coach is No. **375** (**KWE 375D**). It was one of ten in this particular batch (Nos. 366-75 (KWE 366-75D). (*AEC*)

Below: Painted in a unique blue and white livery and subsequently used as a SWFC team coach is No. **376** (**MWA 376D**) which was displayed at Earls Court in 1966. Inside Charlotte Road we see it sporting back to back seating for 28 tables and rear servery, for its football team use. This vehicle was the first Panorama 1 in the fleet.

Above: The 1967 batch of Reliances No. 377-85 (OWA 377-85E) were the last to carry the traditional SUT shield fleet name on their sides. In this view of No. **379** we see the newly introduced and cheap looking squared up fleet name which has replaced the traditional style. It is seen undertaking the Deeside and Scottish Lochs tour.

Below: Sim Rieuwerts was a Dutchman but lived in Sheffield and worked for SUT for many years. His ability to speak many languages was an asset to the company in his role as a courier. He is seen here, second from the left, in dark suit ushering his party of tourists back on board No. **382** (**OWA 382E**) an AEC Reliance with the AH590 engine whilst on the Rhine Valley tour.

Above: This view of No. **381** (**OWA 381E**) was taken just prior to its being destroyed whilst on the Emerald Isle tour in 1970 and shows the clean lines of the Panorama I body. The driver on this tour was Jim Dowling.

Below: The destruction caused by an IRA attack to No. **381** is evident in this photo taken on 7th June, 1970 at Rendon Point , County Kerry, while working the Emerald Isle tour. A local vehicle was hired pending the arrival of a replacement coach, to enable the tour to continue. No. 381 was rebodied with an Elite II body by Plaxton in 1971.

Above: Still wearing the duo green and beige livery of Hirst and Sweeting is **958 EWB**, a Bedford SB5 with Plaxton Embassy coachwork new in 1962. It is on the railway contract and is seen at Sheffield Midland Railway Station looking decidedly down at heel, after takeover by it new owners in 1967. It was withdrawn in 1972

Below: Stopped at the Pilatus Bahn Railway during the Lucerne air/coach tour is No. **386** (**SWJ 386F**) seen in 1970. This batch of Reliances were AH691 engined and featured rather drab 'autumn tint' moquette for 45 passengers. Its courier Roger Tassart is taking a well earned break.

Above: Posing for the camera is Dave Hancock the driver of **391** (**SWJ 391F**) at the Brasserie Continental in Lyon. This was a double-manning tour, in this instance with co-driver Tony Hitchin. (*Dave Hancock*)

Below: At rest before re-commencing its tour of Folkestone is No. **399** (**XWJ 399G**) - the last of a batch of four 40-foot Plaxton Elite bodied AEC Reliance 6U3ZRs delivered in 1969. The others were 396-8. Bill Dickenson is in charge of the blue and grey liveried machine, but it was never used as football transport.

Above: Encountering a bit of a problem on the A1, bound for Scotland is No. **401** (**XWJ 401G**). This was one of four short 41-seat Reliance 6MU3R/Plaxton Elites new in 1969. The overheating front off-side wheel was being attended to by the fire brigade.

Below: This photo of No. **406** (**DWA 406H**) was used as a publicity shot and featured in the SUT holiday brochure of 1971. On board is a complement of SUT staff including driver Jack Bateman. The complete batch was Nos. 404-9 (DWA 404-9H), which were again the Reliance/Plaxton Elite combination. (*SUT*)

Above: Carrying Manx registration **96 XMN** is No. **409** (DWA 409H) which was one of two Reliance 6MU3R delivered during 1970, the other being 408. It is pictured at Tyndwald Hill on the Isle of Man with courier Bert Cubbon. The vehicle was allocated to the island between April 1971 and September 1972.

Below: Just returned to Pond Street, Sheffield after completion of the Blackpool - St Annes - Preston duty is No. **415** (**HWB 415J**) one of five 53-seat 40-footers delivered in 1971. Making up this batch were a further two short, crash gearbox Reliance 6MU3Rs in the form of 410/1 (HWB 410/1J).

Above: The penultimate batch of AEC Reliance 6U3ZR types came in 1973. These were the first Duple bodies for the fleet since 1955, and the first delivered in NBC white to the company, being of the Dominant design. Seen in Blackpool are numbers **429** and **428** (**TWJ 429/8L**) at the Coliseum. The batch comprised ten machines (TWJ 425-34L).

Below: Yes, this is the very last SUT coach. Unfortunately it is in the bland National white livery but did at least carry the legend 'Sheffield United Tours' in red over the front wheel arches. No. **444** was the last of a batch of ten Reliance 6U3ZR Duple Dominant 49-seaters, Nos. 435-44 (AWE 435-40M, AWJ 441-4M).